This book
Belongs to:

_____

_____

To Emma and Eliott.
So that they can always
remember how brave they are.

MG.

A World of
New Beginnings

Melissa Garin

Illustrated by Ale Tadeo

This story begins like many others you may already know,
In a charming little town in the middle of a vast meadow.

What makes this story unique is neither the beginning nor the end,
But the thrilling journey in between, where joy and hurdles blend.

In that charming little town, next to a big apple tree,
Emma and Eliott lived as happily as anyone could be.
Their parents' love and care were treasures every day,
In their little paradise, they loved to run and play.

They had a cozy house with roses by the door,
Their grandparents lived nearby; they couldn't ask for more.

Laika, their furry friend whom they spoiled and adored,
Was always the best companion to snuggle and explore.

Their friends were like family; their bond was tight and true,
They'd be naughty and laugh together, as friends would often do.

Emma and Eliott's lives were peaceful, with much joy every day.
Little did they know that an enormous change was on the way.

One morning, much like any other, they heard their parents' intentions.
"We're moving abroad," said their mother, sparking a million questions.
"Can I bring my teddy bear with us? Will there be treasures along the way?
Do they also have a school bus? Is there a park where we can sway?"

Despite their parents' best efforts, Emma and Eliott felt quite distressed.
As Mom and Dad anticipated their worries, they would gently confess,
"It's alright to be sad or scared. Mom and Dad feel the same way.
Remember, you are not alone. We are here for you every day."

With a lump in her throat, Emma said right away,
"I love our home; I wish we could stay!"

"I see you are upset, and that's perfectly okay.
We will figure this out together," her mom would say.

In the following days, Mom and Dad made them smile,

They showed them pictures of their new place, which had a funny style.

At bedtime, they read stories of other families who had moved away,

And just like you will, they found happiness in a whole new way.

As their house became a maze of suitcases, boxes, and empty aisles,

They bravely wiped away their tears and looked ahead with hopeful eyes.

Emma and Eliott said goodbye to their friends and favorite places.

I won't tell you it wasn't hard to leave all those smiles and familiar faces.

The big day finally arrived when they flew to a faraway land,
They could have never imagined a place so grand.
New people, unusual places, and plenty of things to discover,
There was much to take in; it was a place like no other.

The traditions and even the weather all appeared unfamiliar and strange,
Nothing was like in their peaceful meadow; it was an enormous change.
"It's okay to feel overwhelmed, surprised, or even afraid,
Our differences make us stronger," their dad would wisely say.

At first, it was challenging; simple things became very tough.

Making friends and communicating—the few words they knew weren't enough.

With patience, through signs and gestures, words slowly began to flow,

And as their parents would always say, "Kindness is all you need to know."

There were moments of sadness; to deny it would be a lie.
Sometimes, they missed their old friends and their familiar sky.
But Mama and Papa held them tight through it all,
And before they knew it, their sadness grew small.

In this new world of marvels, they wandered through rare places,
They tried funny-tasting food and learned many new phrases.

The local games were unfamiliar, but they gave them a try.
They asked questions and listened to the people who passed by.

The school was also different, with new lessons every day.
With patience and courage, Emma and Eliott found their way.
Their lives had been transformed, as they would soon discover.
Yet one thing remained the same: their love for each other.

They explored lively cities as well as the countryside,
Taking in the stunning views on this thrilling ride.
They heard bustling streets and felt the ocean breeze on their faces.
In embracing this big adventure, they found joy in all those places.

With each new encounter, their hearts opened wide.
Emma and Eliott made close friends who stayed by their sides.
They found friendship in strangers, a place to call home,
Creating a big, diverse family far from their own.

They faced every challenge together; some things didn't go as planned.
But Emma and Eliott discovered beauty away from their homeland.
In the end, they understood that wherever they would roam,
If they were together, it would always feel like home.

As days turned to months, they no longer felt fear,
In the place they now call home, they had a fascinating year.
From that moment on, with their loved ones by their side,
Moving to new places felt like an exciting ride.

Dear wonderful readers,

Download our FREE COLORING PAGES
and add your unique touch to the story!

Thank you for joining me on this adventure!
If you enjoyed the journey, please consider leaving a review on Amazon.

Your feedback means the world to me, thank you!